The ARCTIC

To Aubrey, with whom I shared howling wolves,
the Midnight Sun, and the haunting call of loons
—W. L.

© NorthWord Books for Young Readers, 2007
Photography © 2007: Wayne Lynch
Map illustration by Mary Jo Scibetta
Designed by Lois A. Rainwater
Edited by Kristen McCurry

NORTHWORD
Books for Young Readers
11571 K-Tel Drive
Minnetonka, MN 55343
www.tnkidsbooks.com

Library of Congress Cataloging-in-Publication Data

Lynch, Wayne.
Arctic / text and photographs by Wayne Lynch.
p. cm. -- (Our wild world. Ecosystems)
Includes index.
ISBN 978-1-55971-960-5 (hc) -- ISBN 978-1-55971-961-2 (sc)
1. Animals--Arctic regions--Juvenile literature. 2. Plants--Arctic regions--Juvenile literature.
3. Arctic regions--Juvenile literature. I. Title.

QL105.L96 2007

577.0911'3--dc22   2006021920

Printed in Singapore
10 9 8 7 6 5 4 3 2 1

Our WILD™ WORLD

ECOSYSTEMS

The ARCTIC

Text and Photographs by Wayne Lynch
Assisted by Aubrey Lang

NORTHWORD
Minnetonka, Minnesota

CONTENTS

"I have many great memories of the Arctic but one that still makes me laugh is the time I caught a bear in a fishing net. I was flying in a helicopter with Peter, a biologist friend who was searching for grizzlies, when we saw a mother bear with two cubs bouncing along beside her. Peter wanted to attach a radio-collar around the mother's neck to track her movements, so he used a dart gun from the helicopter to inject some sleeping drugs into her. When the dart hit the bear's rump she got frightened and ran away, leaving her cubs alone. My job was to help catch the cubs with fishing nets and return the snarling babies back to their mother, who had fallen asleep some distance away. But as soon as the cubs saw us they raced up a muddy valley. We ran as fast as we could, but the bears were faster in the gooey muck. The helicopter pilot herded the cubs back toward us, and Peter and I crouched behind a big rock to wait. When the little bears bounded past us we nabbed them with our nets. This was serious bear research but you couldn't tell it from the way we looked, splattered with mud and each proudly holding our "catch"—squirming, squealing fur balls with needle-sharp teeth. The helicopter gave us a ride back to the sleeping mother bear and the family was reunited. It was just another ordinary day at work for Peter, but for me it was a thrilling arctic experience I will never forget."

THE TOP OF THE WORLD

The Arctic is a magical world of ice, snow, and cold. You might think that such a frozen land would be boring. Never. For more than 25 years, I have traveled to the Arctic almost every year because it is such a fascinating place to explore. I love the people, the land is filled with exciting wildlife, and the seas are decorated with towering islands of ice. There is nothing boring about the Arctic.

The Arctic includes lands from many different countries: the United States, Canada, Greenland, Norway, and Russia.

This book will focus on the arctic regions of the United States, Canada, and Greenland.

Trees often grow along the banks of rivers in the Arctic many miles (km) north of the tree line.

If I asked you to show me the Arctic on a map of North America, you would be correct if you pointed to the top of the map. However, you might have some trouble if I asked you to trace the southern border of the Arctic. Biologists, scientists who study plants and animals, say that the Arctic begins where the forest ends. They call it the tree line. Beyond the tree line, the winters are too long and cold, and the summers too short and cool, for trees to grow. As a result, all the lands north of the tree line have no trees and are considered part of the Arctic. The tree line, however, is not a straight line across the top of North America. In some places, it's far north and in other areas it dips south. If you check the map and start in northern Alaska you can follow the tree line east across the vast wilderness of northern Canada. In the center of the continent, it dips below Hudson Bay, then continues east to northern Labrador on the Atlantic coast of Canada.

The word arctic comes from a Greek word for bear.

When I was a boy, everyone called the native people who lived in the Arctic "Eskimos." In earlier times, these tough people lived in houses made from blocks of snow, called igloos. They invented many things: the bow and arrow to hunt caribou, and kayaks made of animal skins to hunt seals. They were also great travelers and made long journeys over the frozen ocean on sleds they built from animal bones and hides, and they trained strong teams of dogs to pull them. These native people are proud of their early history, but one thing you may not know is that many don't like to be called Eskimos. The word *Eskimo* comes from the language of Indians who lived in the forests south of the Arctic. It means "eater of raw meat." The Indians wanted to insult the Eskimos and make fun of them because they didn't cook their food. Today, most native people who live in the Arctic call themselves Inuit (IN-yoo-whit) rather than Eskimos. In their language, the word *Inuit* means "the people."

LAND OF THE MIDNIGHT SUN

The Arctic is often called the Land of the Midnight Sun. That's because in many areas of the north, the summer sun never sets. It simply circles in the sky, day after day. Since the sun never disappears in summer, no matter what time it is, the sky never gets dark. Even at midnight, the sun shines brightly if there are no clouds. If you want to see the Midnight Sun you must go as far north as the Arctic Circle. This is the name that mapmakers have given to the invisible line that circles the Earth at a latitude of 66 1/2 "degrees" (66 1/2°) North. The city of Fairbanks, Alaska, is just south of the Arctic Circle. At the Circle, the spring days become longer and longer until, for one day of the year, the sun does not set. Usually this happens around June 21. After that, the days slowly get shorter and shorter again until finally, six months later, the day comes when there is no "day" at all. The sun doesn't rise.

The equator is a circle that goes around the widest part of Earth like a belt that goes around your waist. North and south of the equator there are 90 other lines that circle the planet. Mapmakers call these circles lines of latitude. For example, the equator is at 0° latitude, Washington, D.C., is at 39° latitude, the Arctic Circle is at 66 1/2° latitude, and the North Pole is at 90° latitude. Most of the Arctic is between 60 and 90° latitude.

The farther north you go from the Arctic Circle, the more days there are when the summer sun never sets. If you go 100 miles (161 km) north, you will enjoy more than two weeks without any darkness. Farther north yet, in the small Inuit village of Grise Fiord (Grease fee-ORD) in Arctic Canada, the sun doesn't set for almost four months, from late April until late August. The farthest north point on Earth, in the middle of the ice-covered Arctic Ocean, is the North Pole at the latitude 90° North. At the North Pole the sun stays up continually for six months, then disappears for the next six months.

FIORD: a narrow valley that leads to the ocean and is flooded with sea water

Every place in the Arctic that enjoys the Midnight Sun during the summer must pay for it the following winter with an equal number of "Polar Nights," which are days when the sun never rises. So an area that has two months of continuous daylight in the summer will also have two months of constant darkness in the middle of winter. Imagine that!

Scoresby Sound, along the east coast of Greenland at a latitude of 70°, experiences several weeks of Midnight Sun in the summer.

THE BRAVE FEW:
ARCTIC WILDLIFE

Some animals are completely missing from the Arctic. For example, there are no snakes, lizards, turtles, frogs, or toads. The Arctic is just too cold a place for these animals to survive. But that is only half the story. Even though the Arctic may have very few different kinds of animals and birds, the species it does have sometimes occur in great numbers. For example, thousands of seabirds may crowd together on the same cliff in some regions of Greenland, and caribou in Arctic Canada often travel in great herds that stretch as far as the eye can see.

If you study where wildlife lives on Earth you can see a pattern. The greatest variety of animals, birds, reptiles, and insects live in the warm tropical regions around the middle of the Earth. From there, if you travel north toward the Arctic, you will find fewer and fewer different kinds of wildlife until you finally reach the North Pole where there are the fewest of all.

Birds are a good example of this. The tropical country of Colombia in South America has over 1,700 species (SPEE-sees) of birds. If you fly north from Colombia on a trip to the Arctic you pass over the United States, which has roughly 800 species of birds, then to Canada, which has about 400 different kinds of birds. However, most of the birds found in Canada live in the warmer southern parts of the country, not in the Arctic. In Arctic Canada, there are just 110 species of birds, and at the top of Greenland, which is the northern-most land on Earth, there are just 30 different kinds! This same pattern also applies to the mammals, insects, and plants. In fact, no matter which group of living things you look at, the farther north you travel, the fewer and fewer different kinds there are.

These tundra swans have built a large nest of grass and soil in the middle of a tundra lake where their eggs are safe from hungry arctic foxes.

This book is a different kind of nature book than you may have read before. It's a book about an *ecosystem*, the arctic ecosystem. Ecosystem is the word scientists use to describe all of the plants and animals that live together in a community. It is also about how the richness of the soil, the warmth of the days, and the amount of rain and snow that wets the land affect these animals and plants. In an ecosystem, all these things are connected, and all work together. The arctic ecosystem is a story about icebergs as big as buildings, and northern lights that dance across the blackness of the winter sky. It's a story about winter blizzards, treeless land, and bone-freezing temperatures. It's also a story about powerful polar bears, paper-white whales, and great noisy flocks of migrating geese.

MIGRATION: when a bird or animal moves to a new area with the change of seasons

As I write this book it is early summer, and I am packing my bags again for another trip to the Arctic to photograph its spectacular wild animals. I have been a wildlife photographer and nature writer for more than 25 years and I am just as excited to visit the Arctic today as I was for my first trip many years ago. With this book I hope to share with you the beauty of arctic wildlife and the amazing ways in which it survives.

CHAPTER TWO

"The red-throated loon is one of my favorite birds in the Arctic. One summer I found a pair of them nesting by the edge of a lake on a tiny island no bigger than a dinner plate. The top of the nest was just a few inches (8 cm) above the surface of the water and I worried that high waves might wash the eggs away. When the parent loons flew off to fish, I waded out into the frigid water. I raised the nest by tearing chunks of sod from the shoreline and placing them carefully under the two large eggs. It was the best home repair job I had ever done. When the loons came back from the ocean an hour later, they didn't seem to notice the changes I had made and sat on the eggs right away.

Ten days later, there was a big storm with rain and high winds. As I lay in my tent that night I worried about the birds and hoped their eggs would be safe. The next morning when I hiked to the lake, sadly, the loons were gone and the nest was empty. I waded out to see what had happened. Both eggs were resting on the bottom of the icy lake. Large waves during the storm had probably washed them out of their warm nest, which is what I had feared might happen. A week later, I found the loons building a second nest in a better place on the far side of the lake. Birds in the Arctic live with many such problems, and their toughness is one of the reasons I find them so fascinating to study."

TUNDRA TALK

If you ask someone to describe the Arctic they will probably say that it is a cold, snowy place. They are only half right. The Arctic is certainly a very cold place. Winter can last eight to ten months. In many places, there is no sun for long periods of time so it is hard for the land to warm up, and everything freezes. Winter temperatures of -25°F (-32°C) are not unusual. In such weather, the tip of your nose can freeze in less than a minute.

The snowiest places in North America are not in the Arctic at all. Many peaks in the northern Rocky Mountains, for example, get 30 to 40 feet (9 to 12 m) of snow every winter. The snowiest place on the continent is at least 1,000 miles (1,600 km) south of the Arctic in the Cascade Mountains of Washington and Oregon. In the winter of 1998-1999, Mount Baker in the Cascade Mountains of Washington received 95 feet (29 m) of snow—a new record for winter snowfall in North America. That was enough snow to bury three telephone poles, stacked one on top of the other!

The Arctic is definitely a cold place, but surprisingly, it doesn't snow a lot. Forty to 60 inches (100 to 150 cm) of fresh snow a year is usual throughout much of the Arctic. Some places get even less than that. The northernmost part of the Arctic gets so little snow and rain that scientists call it a cold desert. Even parts of the dry Sahara Desert get more moisture than some places in the Arctic!

The Sahara Desert in the winter looks very different from the snow-covered Cascade Mountains.

The cold, dry weather of the Arctic naturally influences the kinds of plants that grow there. While trees don't grow in the Arctic, many plants and bushes are able to survive. Along the southern edge of the Arctic near where it begins, there are thick patches of willow and birch bushes, some of which can grow as tall as a person. As you move farther north and get deeper into the Arctic, the plants get shorter and grow closer to the ground. In fact, most arctic plants grow less than 12 inches (30 cm) tall. Not only are the plants shorter, but they also grow farther apart and are separated by patches of bare ground. In the harshest, most northern parts of the Arctic, no plants can grow at all. The ground is just dirt, gravel, and rock. Biologists use just one word to describe the landscape of the Arctic: *tundra*.

TUNDRA:
treeless plain with only mosses, lichens, and short shrubs growing

The arctic ground squirrel sometimes eats the juicy blossoms of the purple saxifrage as well as the flowers of other arctic plants.

The continual cold freezes the soil, sometimes hundreds of feet (150 m) deep beneath the surface of the ground. Even with the warmer temperatures of summer, which can reach the mid 50s F (12°C), only the top foot (30 cm) or so of the ground thaws out and melts. Deeper down, the earth stays frozen all year round. Scientists call this permanently frozen ground *permafrost*. It is an important feature of the Arctic and greatly influences the plants and animals that live there. For example, the frozen ground prevents plants from growing deep roots. Also, the plants cannot soak up the water they need to grow because most of it is frozen into ice. Permafrost also prevents burrowing animals from digging very deeply, so very few of these types of animals live in the Arctic.

Plants grow poorly in the Arctic, not only because it is cold and dry, but also because there is very little food in the soil for them. When nutrients are suddenly added to the arctic soil the plants grow much greener and thicker. You can see an example of this if you find an old muskox or caribou carcass where the animal died naturally or perhaps was killed by wolves. The remains of the body slowly rot and mix into the ground making the tundra soil richer. The plants use this rich soil for growing. This also explains why arctic plants grow better around old fox dens and eagle perches. Foxes and eagles sometimes drop scraps of food that enrich the soil and make it easier for plants to grow. I have found many arctic fox dens by simply looking for the greenest patch of tundra I could find in the area.

Even though the Arctic is a hard place for wildflowers to grow, several hundred kinds occur in this cold northern area. Most arctic flowers are small and hug the ground where there is less wind and the air is not so cold. Many of them also wrap themselves in fur coats to stay warm, with fine hairs covering their leaves and stems. One of these flowers, called the woolly lousewort, is the hairiest of them all.

I like to lie on the tundra on my belly and use a magnifying glass to get a close look at the bright colors and beautiful designs of arctic flowers such as this lousewort on the right and the arctic poppy above.

ECO-Alert

Even though very few people live in the Arctic, unsafe chemicals from cities and factories far to the south still pollute the water. These chemicals, some of which are very dangerous, drain into rivers, which then empty into the oceans south of the Arctic. The currents in the oceans carry these poisons north to the clean waters of the Arctic where they can make the wildlife sick. If humans are not careful, such poisons may harm them as well.

LICHENS FOR LUNCH

Lichens (LIKE-ens) are found everywhere in the Arctic. They look like small plants attached to rocks, old bones, and caribou antlers. Many kinds also grow directly on the ground. Some lichens look just like splattered blobs of black, yellow, green, and orange paint. Actually, lichens are not plants at all but are closely related to the mushroom, which is a fungus.

Caribou may be the most famous arctic animals that eat lichens. Half of their winter diet is lichens. They sniff the dry, crunchy food under the snow and then dig it out with their front hooves. This winter behavior is actually how caribou got their name. The word *caribou* means "shoveler" in the Micmac Indian language because of the way the animals shovel under the snow to find their winter food.

One of the most common and colorful arctic lichens is the crusty, bright orange jewel lichen. Believe it or not, the jewel lichen grows best on rocks where birds poop. Large birds of prey, such as snowy owls, rough-legged hawks, golden eagles, and gyrfalcons (JEER-fal-cons), often perch on the same rocks day after day to hunt and watch for enemies. While they are waiting, the big birds squirt their white poop over the rocks. Whitewash is a good food for jewel lichens and the rocks soon become painted orange with them.

PREY: an animal that is killed by another animal for food

There are more kinds of lichens in the Arctic than there are kinds of trees in all of the United States and Canada. (Top): The rock wall next to these horned puffins is covered with orange jewel lichen.

ISLANDS OF ICE

To make an iceberg you need only two things: a large glacier that is slowly creeping forward and a nearby ocean. Glaciers are huge rivers of ice that flow like thick, cold toothpaste. The fastest-moving glacier in the Arctic is in Greenland. Its icy nose can grind forward over 2 feet (60 cm) in just one hour. Once a glacier reaches the ocean, the tip of it can break off and float away. These floating pieces of glacial ice are called icebergs.

There are three main iceberg factories in the Arctic: Ellesmere Island in the Canadian High Arctic; Svalbard, an island north of Norway; and Greenland. Of the three areas, Greenland produces the most icebergs. Every year, glaciers in Greenland spill about 15,000 icebergs into the North Atlantic Ocean.

Icebergs vary a lot in size. They can be as small as a refrigerator, called "growlers," or they can be the size of a small house and are called "bergy bits." Some icebergs can even be larger than a 10-story office building. The largest arctic iceberg on record was seen off Canada's Baffin Island in 1882. It was 8 miles long and 3.5 miles wide (12.8 x 5.6 km). That's larger than some towns.

There's a common expression in English, "just the tip of the iceberg," which is used to describe a situation where only a small part of it is apparent. Icebergs are always much larger underwater than they appear at the surface. In general, an iceberg is four or five times bigger below the water than above.

Most icebergs melt or become stuck to the ocean bottom long before they can drift out of the Arctic. In fact, fewer than 1 in 20 icebergs ever floats as far south as eastern Canada. And only 1 iceberg in 140 ever makes it as far south as the eastern United States. It was just such a rare iceberg that collided with the ship called Titanic on April 14, 1912. It was the first voyage of this beautiful ship and it sank in less than three hours, drowning 1,513 passengers.

ECO-Fact

There is very little green on the island of Greenland. The Viking outlaw, Eric the Red, named the island Greenland to trick settlers into believing the land would be good for farming. Greenland is, in fact, mostly ice with a narrow rim of tundra around its outer edge. The ice covering much of the country is 5,000 feet (1,525 m) thick.

THE MYSTERIOUS NORTHERN LIGHTS

On clear nights, the skies of the Arctic are sometimes filled with curtains of green, blue, and red light, dancing across the darkness. The shimmering sheets of colored light may brighten for a time, then fade again. At times, they speed up, then slow down. It almost seems as if the sky is breathing. The ancient Inuit believed that these "northern lights" were the torches of spirits guiding souls to a happy hunting ground in the sky. My grandfather told me they were the reflection of the sun off the ice surrounding the North Pole. Science tells us something different about these mysterious lights, but that doesn't rob them of their beauty. In fact, it makes the display even more exciting to see.

The northern lights are actually caused by invaders from space. The story begins on the flaming surface of the sun, where gigantic explosions occur all the time. The explosions send showers of invisible electrical sparks racing toward Earth at 2 million miles per hour (more than 3 million kph). It takes two days for the sparks to reach our planet, but Earth is not easy to invade. The planet resembles a giant magnet. The force of this magnet surrounds Earth like a blanket and protects it from most of the electrical sparks from the sun. Even so, in the Arctic regions of the planet some of the sparks manage to break through the magnetic shield. As the sparks get closer to the Earth's surface, they collide with the gases in our atmosphere. These collisions, millions and millions of them, produce the colored lights we call the northern lights.

Although I love to watch the northern lights on a black arctic night, it's the wildlife of the Arctic that interests me most. Wildlife in the Arctic lives in three main areas: the frozen sea ice, the rich tundra of the Low Arctic, and the bleak tundra of the High Arctic. In the pages that follow, we'll take a look at the wildlife in each of these three areas. Some arctic animals may live their entire lives in just one area, such as walruses that live only in the icy seas. Others, such as the arctic fox, may wander through all three areas. So, when I talk about an animal in a certain area, that doesn't mean it can't live anywhere else in the Arctic. Each of the wild animals and birds that live in the harsh and beautiful Arctic has an amazing story of survival.

CHAPTER THREE

" I have always had a soft spot for the animals that most people find ugly and uninteresting. In Africa, I love to watch lumpy-faced warthogs rooting in the mud, and in South America, I'm thrilled to find hungry vultures fighting over a smelly dead animal. It won't come as a surprise to you then that I've spent many hours watching wrinkle-faced walruses burping and snoozing in the Arctic. I have photographed walruses in many places in the Arctic but one summer a mother walrus almost ended my photographing forever.

I was in a small rubber boat with two other people and we wanted to get closer to several walruses sleeping on a small piece of floating ice. As our boat drifted closer, one of the calves slipped into the icy water and swam close to us, perhaps to get a better look. I realized that we were suddenly in a very dangerous situation and should move away quickly before the calf's mother showed up. In an instant, she indeed surfaced, then breathed loudly, looked our way, and charged. The two ivory tusks of the angry mother plowed through the water toward us. When she reached the boat she rose up like some giant creature from the deep and smashed the boat's motor with her tusks. I was terrified and yanked on the starter cord of the motor. Thankfully, the engine started quickly and we raced away to safety. The three of us began to laugh as if we were crazy. Not because we thought what had happened was funny, but because all of us were so happy to still be alive. The walrus mother could have easily sunk our rubber boat with her tusks, but we lived to tell another exciting story about the Arctic. "

THE FROZEN OCEAN

T HE ARCTIC OCEAN SURROUNDS the North Pole. It is the smallest ocean in the world. It is so small that it would fit inside the largest ocean, the Pacific Ocean, 17 times! Besides being small, the Arctic Ocean is different from other oceans because it is covered with ice most of the time. Two-thirds of the Arctic Ocean stays frozen all year round. Some of the ice around its edges melts for a few months in the middle of summer. This produces cracks and channels of open water where seals, whales, and seabirds can swim and search for food.

The wind and currents move the sea ice around all the time. Sometimes the ice may move as far as 25 miles (40 km) in a single day.

The moving sea ice is called pack ice. When large pieces of pack ice crash into each other, the ice can pile into hills taller than a telephone pole. Much of the Arctic Ocean is covered with these large hills of ice. When modern day adventurers try to walk or ski to the North Pole, crossing these hills of ice is one of the greatest problems they face. The icy hills, however, are no problem for the great white bear of the Arctic. This is where polar bears live and hunt all year round.

ECO-Fact

Pack ice is different from glacial ice. Pack ice is made from the salty water of the ocean. Glacial ice forms on the land from freshwater and becomes icebergs when it falls into the ocean.

The black-legged kittiwake gets its name from its loud call, which sounds like it is screaming "kittiwake, kittiwake, kittiwake!"

The white beluga whale is well suited to living in the pack ice of the Arctic. It uses its back to break through ice up to 4 inches (10 cm) thick. It can also lift the ice with its back, take a breath in the air space created, then let the ice down without breaking it and continue swimming.

The arctic fox often follows the tracks of polar bears in the pack ice and eats the leftovers from seals that the bears have killed.

ECO-Alert

When humans burn coal, gasoline, and natural gas in their vehicles, homes, and factories, harmful gases escape into the atmosphere and warm it up. In the last 100 years, so many of these gases have entered the atmosphere that the temperature of Earth is beginning to rise. The temperature is rising fastest in the Arctic. Scientists call this global warming. If the Arctic continues to get warmer, the pack ice may disappear. This could mean that polar bears, and perhaps many other Arctic animals, might not be able to survive.

NANOOK

Nanook is the Inuit name for the polar bear, the largest meat-eating animal on Earth. An adult male polar bear can weigh as much as 1,765 pounds (800 kg). Most weigh around 700 to 1,000 pounds (317 to 454 kg) and are taller than the ceiling in your bedroom when they stand on their hind legs. Compare that to the male African lion, which many people call "the king of beasts." The average male lion weighs just 400 pounds (181 kg). Maybe the real king of beasts is Nanook, the king of the Arctic?

This polar bear ate only the fatty blubber and skin of a bearded seal (pictured above) it had caught. The glaucous gulls standing nearby ate the rest.

Polar bears get as big as they do by eating seals, and they catch seals in two different ways: by still-hunting and stalking. In a still-hunt, the bear simply lies on its stomach on the ice next to a seal breathing hole and waits. I have watched a polar bear wait more than two hours for a seal to come up for a breath and then leave when no seal showed up. Every seal has many different holes in the ice where it can breathe. For this reason, a bear must not move around while it is still-hunting or the seal may see its shadow underwater or hear its footsteps.

Stalking is the other way a polar bear hunts. One of the most exciting hunts to watch is when a polar bear stalks a seal that is resting on the surface of the ice. A polar bear may try to sneak up on the seal by crawling over the ice or by quietly swimming up to it. Sometimes several seals use the same breathing hole to reach the top of the ice. When a bear charges a group of seals on the ice, they all try to escape into the water through the hole at once and often the slowest one gets crowded out and caught by the bear. One time, I saw a hunting polar bear dive under the ice and come up through the seal's own breathing hole. To escape, the trapped seal had no choice but to try to squeeze past the bear to get back into the water, and that lucky seal succeeded.

Polar bears usually manage to catch a seal at least once a week. Sometimes, however, when the ice melts, the bears may not be able to hunt for several months. Then, they live off the fat they gained when the hunting was good.

Imagine if you were a mother polar bear that made a den in autumn on the drifting sea ice to have your cubs. When it was time for you to leave your den in April with your newborn cubs the ice might have moved 620 miles (1,000 km) away. That's like going into your house in Washington, D.C., one day and coming out five months later to find that your house had drifted to Florida.

SEABIRD CITIES

Arctic seabirds often nest in huge groups, or colonies. For example, 29,000 screaming pairs of black-legged kittiwakes crowd the ledges of Prince Leopold Island, and 250,000 thick-billed murres (MURRS) bunch together on the cliffs of Bylot Island, both in the Canadian Arctic. These numbers hardly seem like much when you compare them to the 10 to 15 *million* nesting dovekies (DUV-keys), a small relative of the common puffin, which nest in northwest Greenland.

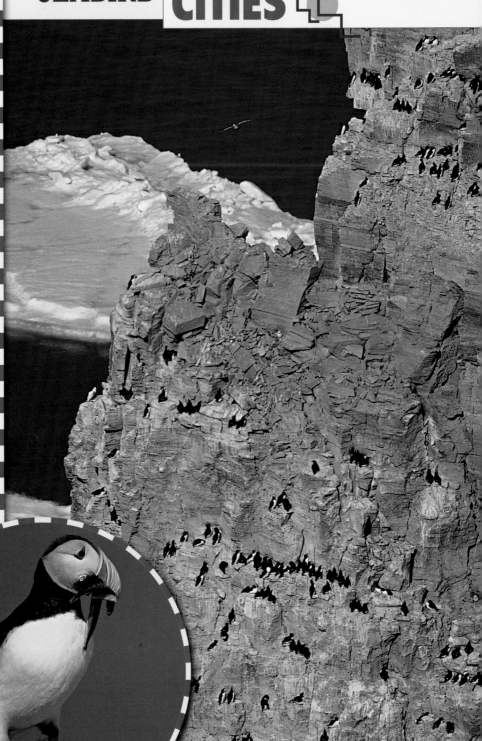

On a single dive, an Atlantic puffin may catch as many as six fish before it comes to the surface for a breath.

Thick-billed murres are nesting on this steep cliff in the Canadian Arctic.

Not many birds can raise families in the difficult conditions of the Arctic. In fact, only about 100 species out of the world's 9,800 birds live there in the summer. Some of the most successful birds in the Arctic are those that feed in the rich waters of the Arctic Ocean. These birds, called seabirds, feed on fish, squid, and other tiny animals that live in the cold, salty water.

When arctic seabirds nest on cliffs away from the water they bring some of the richness of the ocean to the tundra. One of the reasons plants grow so poorly in the Arctic is because there is very little food in the soil for them. Seabirds nesting on cliffs spill some of the food they have brought for their chicks, and they also poop a lot. The poop and spilled food falls onto the tundra beneath the cliffs and enriches the soil so that grasses and flowers can grow there. Afterward, caribou and geese may come to nibble on the plants. In this way, the fish and squid in the ocean, with the help of seabirds, end up feeding caribou. That is the arctic ecosystem at work!

ECO-Alert

In Greenland, some people like to hunt and eat seabirds, especially murres, puffins, and dovekies. They have killed so many birds that many seabird colonies no longer have any birds living in them. When careless people hunt too many birds or animals of any kind, it may take many years for the wildlife to return. Sadly, sometimes it disappears forever.

Dovekies lay their eggs in narrow cracks under large rocks where they are safe from hungry foxes and polar bears.

BLUBBERY BEASTS

PREDATOR: an animal that hunts and kills other animals for food

The big, toothy walrus and six kinds of seals live on the sea ice of the Arctic. The world of ice offers them several benefits. Many arctic predators, such as grizzly bears, wolves, and wolverines, don't usually hunt on the ice, so ice-loving seals are safe from these animals. If the seals rest on small pieces of ice, even polar bears have trouble sneaking up on them. With so much ice, the different seals can spread out and don't need to crowd each other. The ridges and mounds that form in the pack ice also give the seals shelter from strong winds and blizzards. And since pack ice drifts with the currents, it can carry a seal to fresh hunting grounds without the seal having to do any work. Finally, ice-loving seals are always next to the water, so food is nearby all the time.

ECO-Fact

Some arctic seals produce the richest milk of any mammals. The milk of a mother hooded seal may contain 60 percent fat. That's twice as thick as whipping cream! Cow's milk, which you drink, has only 4 percent fat.

Having to sleep on the ice and swim in the Arctic Ocean is a cold way to live. If a person fell into those waters he would freeze to death in minutes. The arctic seals and the walrus have a special way to keep from freezing: blubber. Blubber is fat that covers an animal like a thick blanket. The fat keeps the animal warm and also stores energy for times when food is hard to find. The blubber on a ringed seal can be 2 inches (5 cm) thick. On a walrus, it can be twice that much.

Wolves and grizzly bears will usually not hunt on pack ice so seals are safe from them.

"

CHAPTER FOUR

One of the best parts of Canada is the great wilderness areas in the Arctic. Canadians celebrate their country on Canada Day, July 1, in the same way that Americans celebrate their country on Independence Day, July 4. One Canada Day, my wife, Aubrey, and I were paddling down the Thomsen River in the warm arctic sunshine. We thought it was a perfect way to celebrate our love of Canada, and the day soon got even better. Shortly after we set up camp that afternoon, five white wolves suddenly appeared on a ridge nearby. They stared at us for a few moments, then trotted away as if they had better things to do. As the pack left, one of the wolves lagged behind the rest and howled in our direction a dozen times or more. The howl of a wolf is one of those rare wild experiences that is almost magical. It reaches into your heart and stirs you up with excitement. The wolves that visited us that day disappeared after a few minutes, but the sight and sound of those beautiful arctic animals kept a smile on our faces for many hours.

"

THE LOW ARCTIC

T HE SOUTHERN HALF OF THE ARCTIC tundra is called the Low Arctic. It begins where the forest ends. It is the tundra that is farthest from the North Pole. It includes the northern edge of Alaska, most of mainland Arctic Canada, and the southern half of Greenland. The arctic islands of Canada, as well as the northern half of Greenland, are part of the High Arctic, which we'll look at in the next chapter.

One of my favorite plants of the Low Arctic is the cotton grass. It grows in great meadows wherever there is lots of water on the ground. The cotton grass is probably one of the first plants that every summer visitor to the Arctic learns to recognize. Just search for any plant that looks like grass with a cap of white fluff on the top of each stem. In earlier days, the Inuit used the cotton as a wick for their seal-oil lamps to light the inside of their igloos during the dark winter months. Many arctic songbirds, such as sparrows, longspurs, and redpolls, use the white fluff to line the inside of their nests. Of course the real purpose of the cotton is to help the plant spread its seeds around as they sail away in the wind.

The Low Arctic is slightly warmer than the High Arctic. As a result, the soil unfreezes sooner in the summer creating more water for plants to grow. In the Low Arctic, plants cover more of the ground than they do in the High Arctic and they grow much thicker. Tall bushes, such as willows, alders, and birches, are common. Some of the bushes can grow 16 feet (5 m) tall and may form a thick jungle of branches. The bushes grow especially well along the edges of rivers or in small valleys where the snow piles up in the winter. They are a good place for songbirds to hide from predators and also escape from the cold arctic winds.

DIRT-EATING DALL'S SHEEP

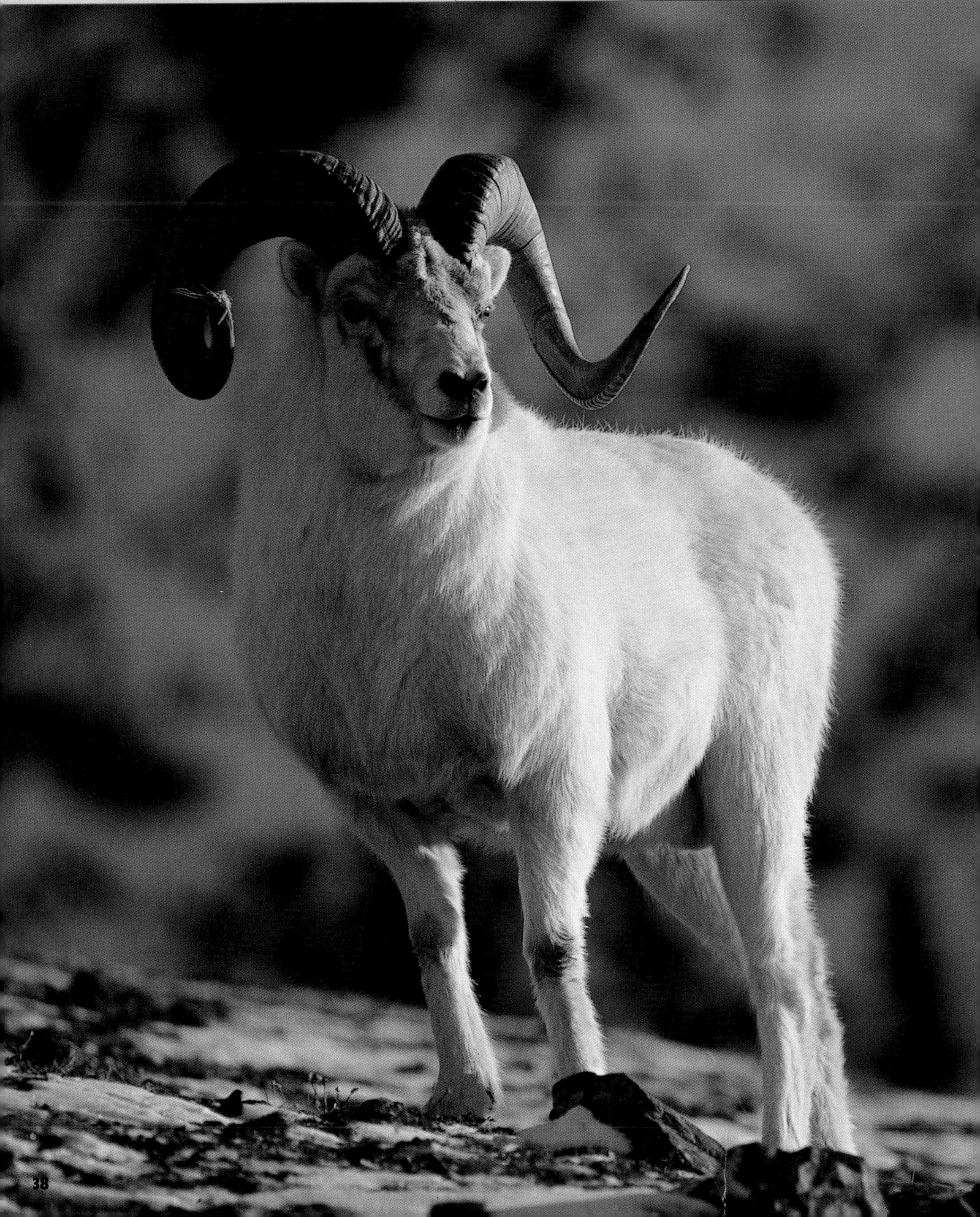

The beautiful white Dall's sheep is found in the arctic mountains of Alaska and the Yukon Territory of Canada. Its fur is white all year round, so in the summer, the sheep are easy to see as they nibble on the grasses of the mountain slopes. Both male sheep, called rams, and female sheep, called ewes (YOUZ), have horns that grow throughout their lives. The horns on the rams are much thicker and longer than those on ewes, and they curl along the sides of their head. In the autumn, rams fight each other by smashing their heads together. The oldest and strongest rams have the biggest horns and they hit the hardest, and usually win the fights with younger males. The winners in these fights get to mate with the females and be the father of many lambs that are born the following spring.

One June, I watched a band of Dall's sheep in northern Yukon make a daily visit to a patch of dry dirt on a mountainside near my camp. With my binoculars, I could sometimes count as many as 30 sheep crowded together on that one small patch of dirt. Each was busy kicking the dirt with its sharp hooves and licking up the loose soil. The sheep came at different times of the day, and usually left after about a half hour. You are probably wondering why a sheep would want to eat dirt? The answer is salt. All animals, including humans, need to eat salt to keep their bodies healthy. During the winter months, the sheep eat dry twigs and grass that contain very little salt, so by the time spring comes they are hungry for a salty meal. Because plants don't have much salt in them, the sheep eat salty dirt instead.

CARIBOU:
THE ARCTIC DRIFTERS

Over a million caribou roam across the tundra of the Low Arctic. In winter, many of them wander into the forests along the edge of the tree line. Here, there are more lichens, grasses, and sedges for them to eat, and the snow is fluffier and easier to dig through with their sharp-edged front hooves.

SEDGE:
a grass-like plant that usually grows in wet areas

When spring arrives, the caribou wander north again in great herds. The pregnant cows lead the way. For them, it is a race to reach the grounds where they will have their calves. Sometimes thousands of mothers trot together in a steady stream.

ECO-Fact

Tuktu (TUK-too) is the Inuit name for the caribou.

The hooves of the caribou spread out and act like snowshoes to help it walk over slippery ice and through deep snow.

The route they follow often changes from year to year. Scientists still don't know why this occurs or how the animals find their way across the flat, treeless tundra. Perhaps the Chipewyan Indians are right when they say, "No one knows the ways of the wind and the caribou."

ECO-Fact

The famous pioneer naturalist Ernest Thompson Seton had a special way to decide which areas in the Arctic had the most mosquitoes. He simply counted the number of bites he got on the back of his bare hand while a friend slowly counted to five. The Low Arctic was the worst place he ever saw. In five seconds, 125 mosquitoes bit his hand.

Most of the calving grounds are windy, elevated places far north of the tree line. Here, there are fewer wolves. It is also colder here, so bloodthirsty mosquitoes arrive later in the summer than they do on the wintering grounds along the tree line. This gives the caribou mothers time to have their calves before the blood-suckers sweep over the land.

Only female mosquitoes feed on blood, but in the Arctic there are millions of them.

In the Low Arctic, mosquitoes often appear in a sudden summer explosion. Open water, long, warm days, and few predators are all factors that help the mosquito population succeed. When this happens, caribou bunch together into groups as big as 20,000. The pestered animals snort and toss their heads. They shake themselves and flick their ears and tail as they walk along, facing into the wind. Eventually, the biting insects are too much to stand, and a few caribou begin to buck and run. Then the entire herd may stampede. Some animals are trampled, and calves are sometimes separated from their mothers. In late summer when the weeks of mosquito madness finally end, the caribou have truly earned the cool, restful days of autumn.

BEAK BUSINESS

Over a third of all the birds that spend the summer in the Arctic are shorebirds. If you have ever visited the ocean you may have seen shorebirds and didn't know those were the small birds running along the seashore in front of the waves, or the different ones probing the mud with their beaks. In the Arctic, the shorebirds include plovers, sandpipers, godwits, phalaropes (FAL-a-ropes), and whimbrels.

When I was a young birdwatcher I wondered why the shorebirds had such different beaks. They often live in the same area of arctic tundra in the summer and eat many of the same insects and spiders. But there are plenty of insects for everyone so it didn't seem that they would need to use their beaks to compete for food. But, in fact, they do. Most shorebirds spend less than three months a year on the tundra. The rest of the year they migrate to the shores of the ocean farther south where there are miles and miles (km) of mud flats. The mud is filled with tasty clams, rag worms, lugworms, bloodworms, crabs, and snails. It turns out the mud flats in the south are where the shorebirds compete for food. That is when the different beaks come in handy, helping them find food in different ways. Longer beaks can reach deeper into the mud. Curved ones can search under rocks, and short, blunt beaks can grab food easily on the surface. Discoveries like this have kept me fascinated with nature for my entire life.

Most shorebirds are plain gray, black, or brown, and although they differ in body size, the biggest difference between them is in the shape and length of their beaks. Some have short, blunt bills, others have slender pointed ones. The godwits have long beaks that turn upward and the whimbrel has a 3.5-inch (9-cm) bill that curves downward.

The Hudsonian godwit screams when a fox comes close to its nest, which is hidden on the ground.

Black-bellied plovers are shy birds whose coloring makes them stand out among other shorebirds.

When thick, gooey oil accidentally spills into the ocean from a leak in an oil tanker, wildlife suffers. It is especially dangerous when it occurs in the Arctic where there is ice almost all year round. The ice makes the oil harder for people to clean up. If a bird gets oil on its feathers it can die because it can no longer stay warm in the cold water. When animals like polar bears lick oil off their fur to clean themselves, they get sick. Whales and seals also get sick when oil gets on their skin and in their eyes.

Newly hatched purple sandpiper chicks crowd under the warm feathers of their mother's belly whenever they get cold.

FOX FEUD

Normally, the arctic fox lives on the tundra north of the tree line and the red fox lives in the forests south of the tree line. In the last 100 years, however, the red fox has slowly moved north and is now a common sight in the Low Arctic. Wherever the two species occur together, the red fox always bullies the smaller arctic fox. The red foxes chase the arctic foxes, steal their dens, and sometimes even kill their pups. Could the adaptable red fox completely take over the Arctic? Probably not, and the reason is body heat.

Animals that live in cold climates have smaller ears, a shorter nose, and shorter legs and tail than their relatives from warmer climates. These are the parts of an animal's body that lose the most heat. The arctic fox, with its small ears and short nose and legs, is much better suited to the cold than the red fox with its big ears and long legs, from which it can lose heat. The fur of the arctic fox is also much thicker than the red fox's. In fact, the arctic fox has the warmest fur coat of any mammal on Earth. So, even though the red fox can live along the edge of the Arctic, there will always be a place for the little white fox.

CLIMATE: the different weather conditions that occur in an area

In summer, the arctic fox sheds its white winter coat for one that is brown and gray.

Both the red fox (right) and the arctic fox hunt seabirds, ducks, geese, and small rodents called lemmings.

This
arctic fox has
heard a lemming under the snow and is
leaping so that it can break through
the thick snow to catch it.

CHAPTER FIVE

"No animal seems better suited to live in the snow and cold of the Arctic than the shaggy muskox. I discovered this for myself one year when I was on a winter camping trip with two Inuit friends. On most of the days, the temperature never got warmer than -13°F (-25°C), which is colder than the freezer in your kitchen refrigerator. Every day we went looking for muskoxen and the ones we watched never seemed bothered by the numbing cold. One frosty morning we found a small herd of four adult bulls in a valley. They were slowly pawing the snow away with their sharp hooves trying to reach the dried grasses underneath. The thick woolly fur on their heads was covered with frost from breathing in the cold air, and small icicles hung from the corners of their mouth where they had drooled and it had frozen. When I drove close to them with my snowmobile, they didn't run. They just stood there boldly, staring at me as they probably had done many times before when hungry wolves threatened to attack them. They were healthy and strong, and their heavy sharp horns were the only weapons they needed to defend themselves. I took photographs of these beautiful animals for almost an hour, and when I left they were still in the valley, scraping food from the frozen tundra."

THE HIGH ARCTIC

THE HIGH ARCTIC IS A COLDER place than the Low Arctic. Because it is colder and receives less snow, there is less water available for plants, making the tundra look different. If you walked from the Low Arctic to the High Arctic you would see a big difference in the plants under your feet. As you moved north, there would be more bare soil between the plants. The plants would be shorter, and there would be no tall bushes as there were farther south.

There are many areas
in the High Arctic in Canada
where there are no plants at all.
The ground is bare soil, pebbles, and rocks
fractured by the fierce cold. Sometimes when
the rocks break apart, they look like a loaf of
bread that has been cut into slices.
Scientists jokingly call these
rocks "troll bread."

The most common things growing on the ground would be lichens, mosses, and grasses. The farther north you went, the fewer wildflowers you would see. However, there is one arctic wildflower that is tougher than all the rest. It's the purple saxifrage and it grows all the way to the northern tip of Greenland, where no others can survive.

The willow is the only woody plant that grows in the tough conditions of the High Arctic. Here, the willows don't grow straight up into the air like the ones you can see farther south. Instead, they grow along the ground like a snake, hugging every dip and crack in the soil. In fact, the willows of the High Arctic never grow higher than 1 to 2 inches (2.5 to 5 cm) above the ground. It's a little warmer close to the ground, and there is less wind to dry out the plant.

The willow is eaten by many arctic animals. Lemmings and arctic hares gnaw on the bark, and muskoxen and caribou eat the twigs and leaves. Ptarmigan (TARM-i-gun), chicken-like birds, nip off the buds. Even humans have a taste for willows. In the past, Inuit children stripped away the outer bark of the smaller twigs and then scraped off the sweet sapwood with their teeth. They called this "eating the fat of the willow."

The buds and leaves of the willows are an important winter food of the willow ptarmigan.

Some arctic willows can live to be over 100 years old even though they never grow more than 3 inches (7.6 cm) off the ground.

BIG BOUNCING BUNNIES

When the arctic hare sees a wolf or other dangerous predator, it does not bounce away with the usual four-legged bunny hop. Instead, it jumps up on its hind legs, sometimes bouncing on its tiptoes. If it decides to run off, it often hops away on two legs as a kangaroo does, with its front legs tucked tightly against its chest. Imagine, the sight of a whole herd of hares hopping off into the distance! Scientists think that the arctic hare hops on two legs to show the predator how strong and healthy it is, and that it would be a waste of time for the wolf to chase it.

An adult male hare is called a buck, a female is called a doe, and a newborn is a leveret.

The arctic hare is the biggest bunny in the world with an average weight of around 10 pounds (4.5 kg). That's almost three times as heavy as the snowshoe hare, which lives in the forests south of the Arctic.

Hares that live in the Low Arctic turn brown in summer to match the color of the tundra. Their brown fur makes it easier for them to hide from sharp-eyed wolves and golden eagles that like to hunt them. Farther north in the High Arctic, hares stay white all year round. There, the summer season is so short that the bunnies don't have enough time to grow a brown coat of fur.

DIGEST: to break down food in the stomach and intestine to release the energy in it

Arctic hares eat grass, flowers, leaves, and twigs. This kind of food is hard for an animal to digest, but the hares have an unusual way to get the most energy out of their food—they eat it twice. You may have seen the dry, round droppings that hares and rabbits leave on the ground when they have been feeding in your family's garden or flower bushes. They also produce a second kind of poop that is soft, wet, and covered with slime. The hares eat these droppings as soon as they come out. They swallow the soft poop whole, without chewing. The poop travels through the animal's intestine a second time and gets digested all over again. In this way, the hare gets as much goodness as it can out of its food. How's that for an amazing survival tactic?

ECO-Fact

Most hares live alone. The arctic hare is different. It sometimes lives in herds. Some of the herds contain hundreds of hopping hares.

THE BEARDED ONE

The Inuit call the muskox *oomingmak* (OO-ming-mack), a word that means "the bearded one." This animal is very special to me and I have searched for them in many areas of the Arctic. One summer, when I was camping in the High Arctic to photograph birds, I often had muskoxen outside my tent. At that time of the year, the bulls travel alone or in small bachelor groups of two or three. They live separately from the females, who travel together with their calves. The female groups are often led by one of the older, more experienced cows. She leads the way when the group must cross a dangerous icy river or move to a new feeding area.

Winter starvation is the biggest danger that muskoxen face. The worst winters are those in which the temperature warms up for a few days and melts the surface of the snow. Afterward, if it freezes again, a thick crust of ice may form on the ground. Even the sharp hooves of a muskox have trouble breaking through the ice to reach the grasses underneath. When this happens, a herd of muskoxen may travel many miles (km) over the frozen ocean to reach other islands where they hope to find food.

Out on the ice, the shaggy muskoxen may be hunted by polar bears. When they are defending themselves against wolves, the animals huddle together in a circle and use their horns in defense if necessary. This probably doesn't protect them as well against polar bears, because the bears are so much bigger and more powerful than wolves. Inuit hunters in Canada and Greenland tell stories of finding muskoxen on the sea ice that were killed by polar bears.

BACHELOR: a male animal that has no female partner

Muskox mothers,
like caribou, have only
one calf at a time. They could not
produce enough milk to feed twins.
Summer in the High Arctic
is often less than three months long.
All muskoxen, including mothers,
must fatten up to prepare
for the long dark winter. Mother
muskoxen could not do this
and also nurse more
than a single calf.

These bulls are huddled together in their defense formation. Later, in the summer, they will likely travel alone and may even fight with each other by ramming heads. When two bulls are getting ready to fight they may roar almost like lions do. Then they face each other and slowly back away, swinging their big heads from side to side. When they are about half a football field apart they charge each other at a full run and smash their heads together. Bulls can head-butt each other as many as 20 times before one of them finally gives up and runs away.

WHITE HUNTERS
OF THE ARCTIC SKY

Two white birds of prey, the snowy owl and the gyrfalcon, hunt in the High Arctic. Both of these are large, powerful predators, but their lives are very different.

The snowy owl is a lemming hunter. An adult may eat four or five of these small rodents a day. In a year, the owl may eat 1,600 of them. The snowy owl doesn't fuss with its food. Just one gulp, and the furry lemming is swallowed whole. One summer, a scientist watched a pair of snowy owls raise seven chicks. He guessed that the family ate more than 2,500 lemmings in just four months!

The number of lemmings that live in a patch of tundra changes from year to year. One year, it may be hard to find a single one. Three to four years later there are many running around everywhere. When lemming numbers are high, snowy owls, rough-legged hawks, and arctic foxes can raise many more young than when lemmings are scarce.

The feet of a snowy owl are covered with thick feathers to keep them from freezing in winter.

The gyrfalcon hunts much bigger prey than the snowy owl does. The bold falcon even tackles geese and sandhill cranes. On the High Arctic islands of Canada, the gyrfalcons hunt arctic hares. In most areas of the Arctic, however, the falcon is a ptarmigan hunter. It chases down its prey with powerful wing beats, then kills it quickly with a bite to the back of its neck. An adult ptarmigan is too big to be eaten completely in a single meal. So, the falcon may share the kill with its mate, or store the extra food for a later meal.

When it comes time to raise a family, the owl and the falcon do it differently as well. The falcon usually lays three or four eggs on the bare ledge of a high cliff. The owl nests on the ground. Sometimes, the snowy owl will lay three or four eggs like the falcon does, but at other times it may lay many more. When lemmings are plentiful and a snowy owl has eaten a lot, it can lay up to 12 eggs. No other bird of prey in the world lays so many eggs at one time.

Gyrfalcons nest on steep cliffs where their eggs and young are safe from hungry foxes and wolves. The snowy owl, by nesting on the ground, seems to be taking a risk with its eggs and chicks. Or is it? The snowy owl is a fierce fighter with large, powerful feet and strong, sharp talons. It does not hesitate to attack foxes, wolves, or ravens. It will also attack curious caribou and muskoxen, or any careless wildlife photographer that gets too close to its nest.

Several kinds of geese in the Arctic take advantage of the snowy owl's fierceness. They build their nests close to the owl family, and the owls end up guarding the geese's eggs as well as their own. If an arctic fox comes sniffing around, the owl quickly drives it away. As soon as the goose eggs hatch, though, the parents quickly lead the goslings away so that the owls don't eat them.

A mother white-fronted goose is incubating her clutch of five white eggs near a nesting snowy owl.

Gyrfalcons may use the same nesting ledge for so many years that the ledge becomes covered with droppings.

ECO-Fact

The Arctic is a good place for geese, and many species nest there. Geese are mainly plant-eaters. Cotton grass meadows and other wet areas provide a good supply of green food for the birds. With so much daylight in the summer, the geese can feed for up to 20 hours a day.

Wildlife lives in a different world than we do. It is a world we are only beginning to understand. I feel very lucky to have been able to return to the Arctic so many times to watch and photograph the fascinating wildlife that lives there. I remember laughing as I watched a Dall's sheep climb along the ledge of a cliff to the nest of a golden eagle and get scared when the tiny eagle chick wiggled its head. Another time, I held a baby polar bear in my lap while some biologist friends examined the young bear's mother. Then there was the summer I spent many days watching a male snowy owl hunt for lemmings and bring the food to his female partner who was sitting on her nest waiting to be fed. Most of all, I will never forget my excitement when a wolverine walked up behind me as I sat on an arctic mountain watching a herd of caribou graze on the tundra below me. These are just a few of the memories I have of the many thrilling days I have spent in the Arctic. I hope some day you also have a chance to hike on the wild tundra and experience its great beauty.

ARCTIC WEB SITES

If you want to learn more about the Arctic and the wildlife that lives there, you can search the Internet for the web sites I have listed below. This is where you can learn about the problems facing the Arctic, what people are doing to save it, and how you can help.

Arctic National Wildlife Refuge (ANWR), Alaska
http://arctic.fws.gov/

Aulavik National Park, Northwest Territories, Canada
www.pc.gc.ca/pn-np/nt/aulavik/index_E.asp

Auyuittuq National Park, Baffin Island, Nunavut, Canada
www.pc.gc.ca/pn-np/nu/auyuittuq/index_E.asp

Dewey Soper Migratory Bird Sanctuary, Baffin Island, Nunavut, Canada
www.mb.ec.gc.ca/nature/whp/ramsar/df02s00.en.html

Gates of the Arctic National Park & Preserve, Alaska
www.nps.gov/gaar/

Ivvavik National Park, Yukon, Canada
www.pc.gc.ca/pn-np/yt/ivvavik/index_E.asp

Kobuk Valley National Park, Alaska
www.nps.gov/kova/

Noatak National Preserve, Alaska
www.nps.gov/noat/

North Greenland National Park, Greenland
http://home4.inet.tele.dk/petersm/albume.html

Queen Maud Gulf Migratory Bird Sanctuary, Nunavut, Canada
www.mb.ec.gc.ca/nature/whp/ramsar/df02s03.en.html

Quttinirpaaq National Park, Nunavut, Canada
www.pc.gc.ca/pn-np/nu/quttinirpaaq/index_E.asp

Selawik National Wildlife Refuge, Alaska
http://selawik.fws.gov/

Sirmilik National Park, Bylot Island, Nunavut, Canada
www.pc.gc.ca/pn-np/nu/sirmilik/index_E.asp

Thelon Wildlife Sanctuary, Nunavut, Canada
www.thelon.com/sanctuary.htm

Vuntut National Park, Yukon, Canada
www.pc.gc.ca/pn-np/yt/vuntut/index_E.asp

Yukon Flats National Wildlife Refuge, Alaska
http://yukonflats.fws.gov/

When DR. WAYNE LYNCH met AUBREY LANG,
he was an emergency doctor and she was a pediatric
nurse. Within five years they were married and had
left their jobs in medicine to work together as writers
and wildlife photographers. For more than thirty years
they have explored the great wilderness areas of
the world—tropical rainforests, remote islands in the
Arctic and Antarctic, deserts, mountains, prairies,
and African plains.

Dr. Lynch is a popular guest lecturer and an
award-winning science writer. His books cover a wide
range of subjects, including the biology and behavior
of owls, penguins, and northern bears; arctic, boreal,
and grassland ecology; and the lives of prairie
birds and mountain wildlife. He is a fellow of the
internationally recognized Explorers Club, and an
elected Fellow of the prestigious Arctic Institute of
North America.

Dr. Lynch has written the texts and taken the
photographs for five other titles in NorthWord's
Our Wild World animal series: *Seals, Hawks, Owls,
Vultures,* and *Falcons.*